My film *Fools Back Out* just wrapped.

Me and the cast are outside saying our final good byes.

After updating everyone's information, I go back to one of the sets.

I say my lines at a table looking up at the different color lights.

I'm dancing on a stage with no audience.

I end with my hands on my hips.

My costar Spencer pulls up a chair and I'm back to reality.

"You enjoying the lights?" Spencer asks.

"Very funny," I say. "I'm gone miss it here."

"Me too," Spencer says. "Even the extras were cool."

"There's nothing like completing a project you worked your ass off on," I say.

Spencer gets behind me and massages my shoulders. "I been feeling you since I first met you," he says. "I didn't want to make you uncomfortable while we were shooting so I never said nothing. You probably think you'll never be as happy as you are right now, but I can make you happier. Can I take you out?"

"I ride solo," I say.

I give the director, Mr. George, a hug. "I need to speak to you in my trailer," he says.

Mr. George goes in his room and I sit next to Lynzey and Lesley from the reality show *The Mendez Family*.

Their sister Lourdes is the most popular. Waitressing with your titties out pays off. She's a model for *The Hottest In* magazine. Her face is on billboards, posters, cosmetics, and clothes.

She's exiting the bedroom with Mr. George.

"Ms. Natalie," Mr. George says. "I wanted to say you did a great job and I'm excited the world is going to be introduced to someone great. Never get comfortable and keep your head on straight. I want a sequel for *Fools Back Out*."

I say thank you and he walks me outside.

A butterfly rests on my hand. Its orange color looks beautiful on my brown skin. It looks at me, then flies away when Mr. George opens the door. "You enjoying my porch?" he asks.

I look at the movie trailers and set buildings one more time before getting in my car.

♥

It's just me, my air mattress, my windows, my computer, and my small TV in my one bedroom apartment.

My check is in the bank. I want to enjoy peace while I'm still not famous.

I put my air mattress by the window and look outside. "Aye Natalie!" Stefan, this teenage boy that lives across the street, yells.

"Take your bad ass inside," I say.

"I'm eighteen now," he says. He's been trying to get my number since he was sixteen.

"Have a good night," I say.

"Alright Natalie," Stefan says.

My phone's ringing.

"Let's go eat," my friend Chasity says. I pick her up and we meet our girls Marty and Marissa at Juliet's Seafood Restaurant.

They don't know I'm an actress. The only people that know are the ones that were a part of the production. I don't want any attention for it right now.

I park next to Marty and Marissa. "Ya'll look good," Marissa says leading the way inside.

I hate when I can't get a booth. "Can we get four shots of

tequila?" I ask the waitress.

"I wish my ass could afford to eat here all the time," Chasity says when we get our food. "I was trying to text you yesterday that I made some steak and potatoes," Chasity says to me. "Then I got a duplicate of the same message."

She sent the message to herself.

"I was gone send you a text saying we made the same thing," Chasity says.

"You should keep shit like that to yourself," Marty says.

I met Chasity at the gym. I knew any minute she would fall or pass out. Without stopping the treadmill she ran to the bathroom and threw up. The staff acted like they didn't see her so I went to see if she was okay. "Damn," Chasity said. "I only had point two miles to go."

She treated me to a burger and fries. We been cool ever since.

I met Marissa at a bar. We were both there alone looking pitiful. I was stressing over being laid off. She was mad because her boyfriend stole her money, phone, and computer.

I met Marty through Chasity.

Lynzey and Lesley are escorted to a long table so they're expecting company.

I don't believe the rumors about the Mendez family being sluts. Sometimes, if you're beautiful, people stigmatize you and assume you're a hoe because some people became successful because they look good and were hoeing.

"Is that them?" Marissa asks me. I tell her yes. She's a fan of the Mendez family.

Marissa's asking Lynzey for a picture.

Lynzey is shaking her head no.

"She want me to catch her on her way out," Marissa says.

Lynzey's mouth didn't move. Lesley was on her phone.

"People been asking me to chill all day," Chasity says. "Had they cooked, I would've been there."

"I'm ready when ya'll are," Marissa says.

"You want to wait for the picture?" Marty asks.

"No," Marissa says.

"We can wait if you want," Chasity says.

"I'm good," Marissa says.

The waiter brings our bill and tells me Shanell Gear wants to talk to me. She's a singer who dates another singer named Troy. I've been following her since she was fifteen.

Shanell gives me a hug and her two friends say hi. I love her pretty brown eyes, perfect shaped nose, and pretty lips.

"I heard about you in *Fools Back Out*," Shanell says. "Most people start off as extras, but you starting in the big leagues."

Shanell's security gets up from the booth behind her. A fan wants an autograph. "I miss when I could go out without people coming up to me," Shanell says. "Enjoy it while it last."

I see Chasity, Marty, and Marissa laughing.

When I sit down, everyone calms down. "Wasup?" I ask.

"We laughing at dumb ass people that wear booty shorts in the snow," Marissa says.

I order a glass of wine.

"Take me to meet Shanell," Marissa says.

"Didn't you already get rejected once?" Chasity asks.

"There will be more people you can get pictures with," I say.

"Marissa it's a name on a sheet of paper," Marty says.

"She wanted a picture," Chasity says.

"I can make a collage at the house," Marty says. Now she's talking about going to her aunt's to chill. She's saying some more shit but I'm not paying attention. I'm looking at Lynzey and Lesley crying and getting their jackets. Their friends put their food in to-go-boxes.

The waiter takes their silverware kits and puts them on another table.

"What happened when I was gone?" I ask.

Chasity, Marty and Marissa say they don't know.

I search Lynzey and Lesley's names on blogs. There's a video of paparazzi asking them questions:

Who did it?

Are you going to sue?

They don't answer.

2

"Let me get that for you." It's Stefan. He puts my trash in the dumpster and opens the door to my building.

I say thanks and take my key back. "You want something to eat?" I ask. He follows me upstairs.

"It's some couches out there on the street," Stefan says. "If you want I can go get you one."

"I don't need no more furniture," I say. "It's only me here."

I make spaghetti and we eat on my air mattress.

"So that's what you want to drink?" Stefan asks before I put the soda in my mouth. He's flirting with me. "Why you smiling?"

"So how's school?" I ask.

"I dropped out," Stefan says.

I never understood why a senior would drop out of school.

"School not paying for shit," he says. "My mom needs help. She's sick and can't work. The landlord don't care. He ready to throw us on the street."

He helps me wash dishes and goes home.

I check my email and the first trending topic is:

Lynzey Mendez tries suicide.

I click the link.

Lynzey Mendez tried killing herself by slitting her wrists. Her brother Lucas walked in the bathroom when he saw blood dripping under the door. He called nine one one. The fifteen year old beauty is recovering at the hospital with her family.

I find a video of Lorena Mendez. "My daughter would never take her life," she says. She'll lie before the dime drops to not lose money.

This is a family that says nothing can tear them apart.

The top comment on one of the blogs says:

I don't get it. The Mendez family have it all: looks and money. What else could anyone want?

Money and looks never could afford happiness.

Shit. I hear gunshots.

Police and ambulances are outside.

I sit on the steps and watch with some other people. I hear gunshots again when the paramedics go upstairs.

Now they're wheeling out a woman. "Ms. Dina!" someone cries. She's Stefan's mom.

They wheel out another stretcher.

"Ma'am you can't walk this way," an officer says to me. I run to the stretcher. It's Stefan. He's been shot. He's not moving and his eyes are closed.

The police put two men in the back of their cars.

3

I go to the hospital to see Stefan and Dina.

"We're going home tomorrow," Stefan says.

He's talking about the same house he was taken out the stretcher on.

"I'll come get you," I say.

"I broke into some people's houses and stole shit. They pulled up when I walked outside and I got jumped until the cops rode by. The officers asked if there was a problem and helped me up. We said no and went our separate ways. Me and my mom got shot thirty minutes later."

He robbed some people that lived down the street from him.

"Least they got them," I say.

"Hopefully they get the other two that was in the car," Stefan says.

I pull up next to a cab at a gas station with Stefan and Dina.

I give Stefan ten thousand dollars. "You know I wouldn't give you no crooked ass money," I say.

"Help me," Dina says. She's holding her stomach, which is why she can't work and Stefan is out robbing people.

"If you ever need anything, I don't care what it is, I'll do it," Stefan says.

4

It's time to move.

My house needs a gate and security system.

I pay cash and get the keys to the first house I see.

I'm shaking my ass and drinking around my mansion in a bikini.

I open the windows and put some music on.

I have a house party by myself.

Someone rear ends me and keeps going on my way to get black and pink paint.

When they park, I write down the license plate.

When they get out the car, I take a picture.

"I'm sick," I say. Marty's on the phone. I don't want any questions about anything so she can't come to the mansion.

I'm painting my girl crush, Melissa Brown. She's the first girl I ever wanted to date.

I paint her hair black and shirt pink. Everything looks perfect on her.

I look at pictures on LuxuryPosts.

I put the painting of Melissa in a frame with pink lights around it and draw another one.

5

I can't be on screen looking good and go to an interview fat as hell.

Natalie McIntyre refuses to be that bitch.
After three laps around the house I sit on the front porch.
Before I get online, Marty calls.
"How you gone move and not tell nobody?" Marty asks.
I hate when people show up unannounced. Every time someone calls me I give them an excuse. I can do everything I want without leaving my gate.
I don't want to go nowhere.
"I been stressed," I say. "I'm in Victorville."
I'm in Hollywood.
"Marissa going out there next week," Marty says.

6

Marty's in the dressing room, Marissa had to work and Chasity's next to me.

Marty's sucking her stomach in to fit in her jeans.

I give her a bigger size.

I'm looking at heels and Marty and Chasity are looking at boots when someone gets caught stealing.

Spencer is walking in. I hide behind a clothes rack. I'm walking sideways to keep an eye on him and get to the door. Marty and Chasity are looking at me crazy. Spencer starts talking to a worker and I go to the bathroom and move the cone out the way so the door can shut.

Spencer will bring up the film.

"What's wrong with you?" Chasity asks.

"My stomach started acting up," I say. "Where's Marty?"

"In the store," Chasity says.

"Let me use the bathroom while I'm in here," I say. I let a couple minutes pass.

"Girl how much soap do you need?" Chasity asks. I squeezed the dispenser six times. "You okay?" I rinse my hands off.

Marty is talking to Spencer in the store.

"He's nice," Chasity says. She takes a picture of Marty and Spencer.

I go to another store.

Spencer comes up to me while I'm looking at clothes. "What's going on with you?" he asks.

"I don't want them to know about the film yet," I say. "I don't want that shit spreading. Look at you in your hat and glasses hiding from every girl you don't want to come up to you."

"They already know," Spencer says. "Chasity asked me to meet one of her best friends, Natalie. She said to make her feel special and call her Ms. Natalie McIntyre. I described a girl that I worked with on a film called *Fools Back Out* and what do you know, she appeared. Sorry," he says and walks away.

"Shit, I'm not hungry no more," Marty says.

"I'm sorry," I say. "I didn't want it to get around. I wanted to be regular until it was released. I was at the park watching some men play basketball and one of the players gave me a business card. He told me to email his dad George. I did and I got the lead in *Fools Back Out*."

"You thought you couldn't trust us?" Chasity asks. "We would've bragged about our girl getting the lead in a film."

"If you didn't tell us not to," Marty says.

"I'm sorry," I say.

"This why you haven't been inviting us over too huh?" Chasity asks.

"Forget that," Marty says. "You like our sister. You don't have to keep nothing from us."

"I live in Hollywood," I say.

"So I came out here for nothing?" Marty asks.

After painting Melissa, I call Chasity and it's loud as hell in the background.

"Who you with?" I ask.

"Marty and Marissa," Chasity says.

"Ya'll want to come by?" I ask.

"Is it alright if we bring some people with us?" Chasity asks.

Damn. I lied about where I lived and didn't say nothing about the movie. Not the damn apocalypse.

7

Chasity introduces me to Trish and a cute ass Latino, Amber.

They been drinking. Amber, Marty and Marissa can't walk up the stairs straight.

"I wish my mom would've left me a mansion when she died," Trish says. Chasity told her that lie.

"She's not dead," I say. "She moved."

We take the pizza, chips, salsa, and drinks to the backhouse.

Trish and Marty roll blunts and I turn the music on.

Me and the girls take a shot and get high.

Marissa takes pictures and puts them on LuxuryPosts.

I go inside to grab my phone and get on Amber's LuxuryPosts page. She's a model.

Trish jumps in the pool topless.

"Natalie come hit this," Chasity says.

"I'm faded enough from the drinks," I say still hitting it.

Marissa, Amber and Marty are in the pool sharing a blunt.

"My nigga where the rest of the liquor?" Amber asks drinking out the bottle.

I tell Chasity to walk with me to get another bottle. "Don't bring that nigga saying Latino around me no more," I say when we get in the kitchen. "You know them girls that be trying to act like, what they think is black, get on my nerves. She not that faded. I hate stupid tramps like her."

"It's your house," Chasity says. "You want her gone tell her."

"I don't need to tell her," I say. "Just don't bring her back and let me know when you invite her anywhere so I don't come."

Everyone's gone when I wake up and my front door is open.

I clean up the broken glass and food on the floor. I was too faded to remember how this shit happened.

Fuck. I didn't have the cameras on.

My room with the Melissa paintings is open. The lock is broke and the key is on the floor.

I take a shot.

I ask Marty, Chasity and Marissa who broke the lock on my way to our dance practice and they all don't know. "Who left my house last?" I ask. "The door was opened." They don't know.

Marty calls Amber and Trish. They don't know.

When I walk in the theater, a casting director says everything's behind schedule. "Is it alright if we use the audience to finish up?" he asks.

I have rehearsal with my dance crew, and his people are rehearsing lines.

"Sure," I say. They go to the back.

Me, Chasity, Marty, Marissa and four other girls are practicing for the Song and Dance Awards. I'm nominated for an award for creating the choreography and my crew was invited to perform.

The casting director and his crew are done but still watching us.

We show the fuck out on stage.

I drink and edit the clips of my dance crew's last five practices and post them on LuxuryPosts.

Me and Amber's names are trending. I go to the trending topics because Amber blocked me on her page. Amber and her fans are putting pictures of my head on animal bodies and posting statuses: *Will Natalie just die? Nothing ass women.* Amber is calling me evil, ugly, and mean. She's saying I'm worthless and hate her because she's beautiful.

I go on blog sites looking for answers.

I drop my cup when I read a status Amber deleted: *Natalie called Melissa a bitch and whore. She said she's not good for anything but being a lying bitch and breaking up happy homes. Natalie said Melissa is lying about the child. It is hers and not her sisters.*

This bitch wants to die!

I pour some more liquor and call Chasity. "What's going on with Amber?" I ask.

Chasity says she doesn't know. I hear people whispering in her background.

"You see what she saying about me?" I ask.

"Yea," Chasity says.

"Why the fuck is she acting like that?" I ask. She says she doesn't know.

She also says she'll call me back and never does.

Amber posts: *I was hacked.*

8

I hire a personal boxing trainer to release the anger Amber put in me. His names Allen. He's fine as hell.

"You ready Ms. McIntyre?" Allen asks.

"I need to stretch," I say.

Allen holds the punching bag and I let loose.

"Who's the boyfriend you want to fight?" Allen asks.

"No boyfriend," I say. "Just stupid ass, childish bitches."

"I'm sorry," he says. "I get a lot of women that come to prepare for they man."

We do pushups on mats in front of the mirrors. After five I fall on the mat. "It's when you feel like you can't take anymore that you should keep going," Allen says. "It'll build your strength."

"Can you get me some water?" I ask.

"I don't think the water fountain will work if I bring it over here," Allen says.

I get some water and sit next to the fountain. Allen sits next to me and we watch an old lady box a man in the ring. "You want to get in?" Allen asks.

"I'm hurting all over," I say.

I still try punching the bag a few more times.

"When will I see you again?" Allen asks.

He's attracted to me.

I'm attracted to him too.

"I'm not sure," I say.

9

I'm painting Melissa and drinking wine trying to swipe my mind of the public humiliation that Amber caused. I want to beat her fucking ass for saying I said that bullshit about Melissa.

I want to beat her fucking ass for bringing Melissa in this.

I'll be seeing a massage therapist soon.

I'm back at the boxing ring. Not to develop more skill but to develop me and Allen's friendship.

"You tired already?" Allen asks. I'm hitting the bag so weak it won't move and he not even holding it.

"I need to sit down for a minute," I say.

We sit on the bleachers.

"You can talk to me," Allen says.

"I kept some shit from my girls, and now I'm paying for it," I say.

"Girlfriend?" Allen smiles.

I throw my towel on his face. "I'm not gay," I say. He folds the towel and wipes my face. "I didn't tell them I moved, and some other shit, because I wanted to hide something for as long as I could. They found out from somebody else and now they leaving me out. I thought we made amends at this party I threw, but I guess not."

"Was that your first time keeping something from them?" Allen asks. I say yes. "I'm going to be real with you," he says. "That don't matter. If you lie once people going to question everything you ever told them."

"Thanks," I say.

"So you want to get back to the bag or what?" Allen asks. I say no. "Can I take you to get something to eat?" he asks. I say yes.

We go to a restaurant around the corner. I order pasta and he gets wings.

"Can you at least act like you're happy to be here?" Allen asks.

"Sorry," I say. "I just can't believe how one day I woke up on cloud nine and the next day dropped to ground zero." Allen chokes on his wing.

"I'm not laughing at you," Allen says. "I think that was a good way to describe how you feeling."

"I guess I feel guilty," I say. "Enough about me. Let's talk about you. Do you always invite your clients out to eat?"

"No," Allen says. "I've never had a client as beautiful as you. You have a nice personality, good conversation and you're smart." I say thank you.

He sits next to me and we feed each other.

When I get home, I walk around in lingerie and heels.

10

I'm watching The Celebrity Gossip Station. An actor is getting bombarded by a bunch of fans and someone that doesn't like him spits in his face. *Fools Back Out* is coming out soon. I need to hire a bodyguard.

Thirty two people show up for the job. One man says he can only work for two weeks. He only needs a temporary job because he's starting back at the oil refinery soon.

The man walking in right now, he has titties. "What's your name?" I ask.

"Briana, but call me Brian," she says. Her voice is deep.

"Okay Brian," I say. "What experience do you have protecting people?" I want to ask if she is a man or woman. If he was born a boy, girl, or both.

"I grew up in the projects and fought bitches off my sisters and brothers all the time," Brian says. "I never lost."

That's just the type of hood rat answer I was expecting from this boyish girl.

Hell no I'm not hiring his or her ass.

"I'll contact you tonight if I'm interested," I say. Out she he goes, and in walks someone that fits the build that I want.

He has muscles.

He hands me the paper I requested with all his information.

Brian didn't so I can't contact him or hers anyway.

"Tell me about yourself," I say.

"I'm thirty years old," Grant says. "I was a security guard at the mall. I wanted to do something different so I started bodyguarding. When I'm not doing that, I'm at my dad's clothing factory."

He's the first person to have bodyguard experience.

"Are you willing to take a bullet for me?" I ask. A bullet guarantees time in a hospital, internal damage, and could take his life. I need to know if he's willing to die for me. That's the ultimate sacrifice. He says yes. "How do you train your mind to put your life before a complete stranger? What about your kids and girlfriend? Don't they have a problem with you willing to die for someone that's not in your family?"

"I don't have kids or a girlfriend," Grant says. "If I did I wouldn't take a bullet for no damn body. One day I was walking down the street with a friend. As soon as shots started firing someone pushed me to the ground and stayed on top of me. He told me to close my eyes. I did what he said. The old man's blood started dripping on me. I tried getting up but he was too heavy. The police lifted him off. He was dead. And so was my friend. To this date I don't know why he saved my life. But he inspired me to take this job."

His story is the most touching one I've ever heard.

I call Grant before I go to bed and tell him what I'm expecting of him. "I like to get what I came for and leave," I say. "If someone spits on me, throw him across the room and make his head hit the wall so hard that it knocks some sense into it and he regrets what the hell he did."

11

I'm on Melissa's LuxuryPosts account. She's still denying rumors that Nick is her child because she's embarrassed the baby daddy is in prison for murder. She tells people it's her sisters. Melissa told people she was pregnant before her baby daddy killed.

I hang my fifteenth painting of Melissa next to another one of her and watch one of her films called *I Need a Dime* under my Melissa blanket.

My mom wants to have a family outing. She says we need to do something else besides have dinner.

I have a brother named Nathan and a sister named Natonya.

I haven't told them about the film because everyone in my family talks too much. They think I'm still working at Benny's Madre, a Mexican restaurant.

After standing in line three hours at the amusement park, my mom says she'd rather cook. We make fried chicken, corn on the cob, greens, and mashed potatoes at her house. Nathan could at least be shaking the chicken in the bag of flour. He's playing video games.

"How's work at the casino Tonya?" Mom asks.

My heart started beating fast when she said work.

"It's alright," Tonya says. "I still get the discounted food. A couple more years and I'm headed to Dubai."

"Why Dubai?" Mom asks.

"It's pretty and I want to move," Tonya says.

I can't think of anything to say so I pour some water and drop the cup on the floor.

"Towels are in the hall closet Natalie," Mom says. I clean up the water.

Instead of going back in the kitchen I go in Nathan's room. I need to give Mom a few minutes to think of something else to talk about.

"Wasup little brother?" I ask.

"Nothing but school," Nathan says. My brother doesn't talk much. At least not to me, Mom and Tonya. He always gives us short responses. Not wanting to bother him I scope out his room. "Get out my drawer," Nathan says.

"Why? What's in it?" I ask.

"None of your business. Go finish cooking," Nathan says.

"What? Go fishing cooking?" I ask. "What you got in your drawer, condoms?" I ask.

"No," he says. "And don't say that no louder."

"Are you having sex?" I ask.

"No. Go finish cooking," he says. I don't move so he tickles me.

"Nathan and Natalie come eat!" Mom yells.

Dinner's going good until Mom brings up Dad.

"Your dad wants to be around you guys," Mom says. We know she lying. She likes to hear that we don't like him because she don't. Edmond left when Mom got pregnant with Nathan. He didn't want anymore kids. He heard child number three and disappeared. He only called on our birthdays so me, Tonya and Nathan changed our numbers. It hurt more to hear from him once a year than it did not to hear from him at all.

We're not a very social family.

"What's going on with you and that model Amber?" Tonya asks when we get outside.

"She was hacked," I say.

"You don't believe that shit," Tonya says. "I'll beat the fuck out of that bitch."

12

I'm at Allen's house.

He's making pasta.

His paintings look awful and have signatures. They're from an art gallery. They should be in a shed. My Melissa paintings are better.

"Do you like the paintings?" Allen asks. I say yes.

"Water, juice or soda?" he asks. "I have wine and liquor too."

He makes us wine and we walk outside while the foods cooking.

"It's peaceful out here," I say.

"Everyone keeps to themselves," Allen says.

The lady that jogged past us is holding her leg and screaming.

The ambulance arrives.

Allen feeds me pasta. "I used to be a chef," he says.

"What happened?" I ask.

"I can play chef any day," he says. "Do you have a man?"

"If I did I wouldn't be here," I say.

He spreads my legs and eats me.

13

I'm at my costar from *Fool's Back Out*, Jamal's, mansion party.

There's people at the bar.

I'm leaving before they get on the road.

"You look good," Jamal says walking by with his friends.

I go to the kitchen and see Melissa, Lina Mendez, and their best friend Erica coming in the house.

I grab a drink.

Lina, Erica and Melissa get in the pool. Melissa looks good in her blue bikini.

"Melissa is good eye candy, huh?" the man next to me asks. "I'm Arnold."

He's fine as hell.

I wish he wasn't gay.

I go sit in the den and wave to Melissa, Erica, and Lina.

Lina whispers in Melissa's ear and Melissa gives me the middle finger. She has pictures on LuxuryPosts sticking her middle finger up. It's something she does.

Lina's rolling her eyes at me.

I'm almost to my car. I hear someone driving towards me.

It's Lina, Melissa, and Erica. Lina's jerking her car at me. Melissa is laughing and Erica is taking pictures.

"Stop!" I scream.

Lina won't.

"Nigger," Lina says.

I'm on the freeway. Lina, Melissa, and Erica are sticking their middle fingers up. Lina's honking her horn and tailgating me. I speed and lose them.

They find me.

Lina's honking.
I take the streets home.
I have a cop following me.
I get a ticket.

14

I'm at dance rehearsal.
 The *Song and Dance Awards* is coming up.
 The routine is solid.
 We're ready to go.
 Everyone says bye to me except Chasity, Marty, and Marissa.
 Friends come and go.
"Hi Natalie," Mr. Terrance, the producer of the show *Model's Run It* says when I get outside. "Got a moment?" I say yes sir. "I want to put on a show. I want it to be creative with lots of different talent. You're multitalented and you look amazing. You are the complete package. I want to put on a modelling show that's never been imagined. Thirty grand." I say yes.
 He gives me the details.
 The shows airing on The DPN: Darla Penn Network.

 I'm in my office planning *Model's Run It*. The show will include modeling, fashion, dancing, singing and acting.
 The models will have dancers enhancing everything they do. The singers will have actors enhancing their words. I will have everyone's pictures and names floating through the audience and on the screens. The host will be on point.
 The hottest females to walk the planet will be in the show.
 There will be effects. Flashes will go with the choreography and screen clips. Clothes will light up. There will be laser lights, fog and wind machines, and tributes to deceased artists.

I hire an assistant. Her names Tori.

I tell her to call Lorena and see if I can get Lynzey and Lesley to model. Fuck that shit with Lina. "You know they talking shit about you on the internet?" Tori asks. I check the blogs. Lina posted a video of a dog shitting on a shirt with my face on it and Lourdes, Lynzey and Lesley reposted it. Lesley posted a video of a kid burning my shirt.

They said they were hacked.

"What the fuck is wrong with them?" I ask.

"I was hoping you could give me the inside scoop," Tori says.

I get on Lina's LuxuryPosts page and there's a group photo of her, Erica, Melissa, Chasity, Marissa, Marty, and Amber.

15

I'm guest starring on The Yoop's House.

Over the break I record a video. I'm shaking my tripod because the damn wind keeps blowing it. "You want some help?" a beautiful woman asks me. I say yes. "I'm Latoya."

"Natalie."

Latoya is a hero.

"I owe you one," I say and give her my number. "Anything you need, don't hesitate to ask."

"Anything?" Latoya flirtatiously asks.

When I get home Latoya gives me a call. It's her birthday and she's going to Empire Nightclub.

I hire a photographer.

I want pictures and footage with Latoya. She is flawless.

We're in a booth in the middle of the club that's a few feet above the ground. Melissa's giving Latoya a hug and coming to the table.

Shanell has everyone sing happy birthday to Latoya.

We go to the VIP section, dance and take shots, then go outside.

Shanell's fans are trying to hop the gate.

A limo pulls up and Shanell and her crew get in. Latoya tells me to follow them. "Ride with her," Latoya tells Melissa.

"We were drunk," Melissa says on the walk to my car. "We got a lot of shit that's fucking with us. And fuck our dumb ass statuses. Can I do anything to make it up to you?" She kisses me on the cheek. "How long before we get to the car?" she asks.

"We're almost there," I say.

"How long is almost?" Melissa asks.

I point to my car in the parking lot I'm turning into.

"You better be a good driver," Melissa says.

"I'm an excellent driver," I say.

"What's so funny?" she asks.

"Huh?" I ask.

"You holding in your laugh," Melissa says.

"This lady thought she was on tonight," I say.

"Oh I see. You think because you're a good dancer you can laugh at everybody else," Melissa says. I'm not telling her I'm happy it's just me and her. "Toya said you was alright," she says.

"How long does it take to get there?" I ask.

"Twenty minutes," Melissa says.

I get in the carpool lane and turn on the radio.

Shanell's house is a damn city. We're in the backyard drinking, smoking, eating and watching music videos.

Shanell gives Latoya a stack of hundreds and two rolled blunts and passes one to me.

When I get home I make a sandwich, grab a pickle and paint a portrait of Melissa and Latoya together.

16

Me and Latoya are downtown.

"How does it feel to be twenty seven?" I ask.

"Like I'm going to tell everybody I'm twenty one from now on," Latoya says. "Times going by too fast for me."

"Me too," I say. "Seems like yesterday I was getting a cap and gown."

There's people popping and locking. I put a dollar in the bucket and Latoya comes back to my house.

Every time I post a picture of me and Latoya on LuxuryPosts, Shanell posts a picture of her and Latoya.

I'm happy Latoya's lying in my bed.

"You can lay next to me," Latoya says. I'm on her LuxuryPosts page. She's a judge on a show called *I Surrender*.

We watch a movie. I get a blanket and she puts it over both of us.

Now she wants something to drink.

"You couldn't have asked that when I was up?" I ask.

I bring out wine.

"Girl go get us some liquor and shot glasses," Latoya says. "And bring the bottle of wine back!" she yells.

I smell the weed walking back to my theater.

I hear music.

Our movie night turned into a party.

Latoya sits me on her lap and we share a blunt. I give her a lap dance. We share a wine glass. She kisses me. We take shots. She grabs my ass and eats me.

I return all the favors that she gave me.

I ride her face and she smacks my ass.

She wiggles the cheeks.
She massages my pussy.

Tori picks me up after rehearsal for *Model's Run It*.
I like this Dalton Win song until he says:

One day I want to see someone burn in hell fire.
Hopefully her name is something like Natalie McIntyre.

Dalton is Lina's boyfriend.
"You really need to find out what them bitches problem is," Tori says.
I call Latoya and get two beeps.
I send her a text and get an error message.

Lights get low and the music begins. My dancers rise up and explode into the choreography. Lights flicker and the wind machines hit right. The pictures and live footage are on the screens.
My host welcomes everyone and dances.
Me and my dancers take the stage and kill the choreography while the models walk.
I come out again and the models walk with angel wings.
I have models dancing and walking the runway while my headliner Marsha Neals sings.
The bikinis match the laser lights that are flashing. The red dresses that light up with the fire effects are on.

Model's Run It is a success.

My phone rings early as hell. I hold down the end button.

It rings when I turn it back on. "Is this Natalie McIntyre?" a boy asks.

"Who is this?" I ask.

"You're number one fan," he says.

"Can you please tell me how you got this number?"

"Someone posted it online," he says.

"What's your name?"

"Timmy," he says.

"Timmy, I have to go," I say.

I type in half of Latoya's number on my other phone and delete it.

I put star sixty nine in front.

Someone's laughing in the background when she answers the phone.

"See if she said anything on LuxuryPosts," I hear Melissa say.

I say hello and Latoya hangs up in my face.

I go to a soul food restaurant.

Lina walks in the door and is trailed by Melissa, Erica and Lourdes.

Lourdes requests to sit behind me.

"Sweety what's your name?" Lourdes asks.

"Ebony," the waitress says.

"Do you want an autograph?" Lourdes asks. Ebony nods her head quick. "Get me something to sign."

"So how did it feel convincing Mom not to let Lynzey and Lesley attend that awful fashion show?" Lourdes asks Lina.

"Good," Lina says. "No one could eat and watch that shit."

I'm laughing.

She's the heaviest in her family.

"I know that ugly bitch isn't laughing at me," Lina says.

"You want to tell me what the hell I did?" I bitterly ask. "Melissa are you fucking bipolar?"

Lina pours my water on me. I try to get up and she pushes me back down. Melissa pushes my head. Lina grips my knife and says, "Don't ever mess with my family again."

"I don't know what you're talking about!" I yell.

"Fuck you," Lourdes says.

I hit up Jamal for some cocaine.

He got arrested for it being found in his car twice.

It's simple.

He's rich and famous.

"Is this your first time?" Jamal asks. I say yes.

He demonstrates.

I try.

This will be a new practice of mine.

Jamal leaves and I invite Grant over. His smile turns into a frown when he sees me. I fall. Grant puts me on the couch.

"Why the fuck are you taking this shit?" Grant asks.

"What shit?" I ask.

"The shit that has your eyes fucked up," he says. "The shit that's gone fuck up your life. I been around crackheads before."

"You sound like my daddy," I say and hit my knee on the table. "Help me."

"No keep falling," Grant says.

"You don't know shit about me Grant," I say.

He sits next to me on the floor.

"Help me get to know you," he says.

I was inviting him over to fuck.

We don't.

He stays the night and vents in the morning.

"You worked for all this and that shit gone make you lose it," Grant says. "Don't use that shit no damn more. I can get you where you want to be without that shit."

"Keep your word," I say.

"I want to hear everything," Grant says undressing me.

He kisses, bites and sucks on my ass.

He eats me.

He puts his dick inside of me.

I'm at Natonya's house babysitting my nieces Denise and Rhea. I take them to the park and treat them to ice cream, then we go back to their house and sleep.

Natonya wakes me up when she opens the door.

She's in her room smoking a cigarette. I open the windows and put my shirt over my nose.

That shit don't work.

I sit by the window.

Natonya's mad she couldn't kick it with her baby daddy because he got other shit going on. That other shit is his wife. She will be smoking all night.

I'm gone.

17

I treat two of my dancers, Sky and Jamie, to Shanell's concert. I bought the tickets a while back.

After a few verses Shanell stops.

Security tells me, Sky and Jamie we have to go.

Me and the girls chill at my house.

Jamie's opening the liquor bottle.

"Shanell and Lina saying you had a threesome with Allen and Grant," Sky says.

"They nosy hoes," Jamie says.

Allen and Grant are at my house. I need to kill these rumors.

"You got us sitting in here and you haven't introduced us," Allen says.

"Allen this is Grant. He's my bodyguard. Grant this is Allen. He's my boxing trainer," I say.

"I take it you're fucking him too?" Allen asks.

Grant gets up. "Call me when you need me," he says.

"Damn. If he stayed you would've been set. I heard you like yours with two," Allen says.

Me and Tori are at the *Song and Dance awards*.

Shanell's wearing a shirt that says *I am Natalie* with me in fire on the red carpet.

"When do we go on?" Chasity asks with Marty and Marissa on her sides.

Me and my crew tear the stage up.

Shanell presents the best dancer award and I win. I walk on stage happy I won but even happier Shanell has on a dress and not that shirt of me.

My award is on the floor next to the microphone.

Shanell kicks it when I try to pick it up.

I get it on the second try.

I find Shanell after the show and bump her shoulder so she turns around. "What the fuck is wrong with you?" I ask. I put my award down and her security stands in front of her.

"It's paid for the night. Go wherever you want," I tell Tori when I get home.

I hit up Jamal for crack.

I can't become an addict.

I buy shit for a photography studio. I put a picture of my equipment on LuxuryPosts.

I release the video of me dancing that Latoya recorded and remind her I owe her. She says she needs a favor for her sister.

I set up in her backyard.

We were supposed to start thirty minutes ago. I knock on the screen door and hear shower water. I get on Latoya's LuxuryPosts and see a picture of her and Melissa with the caption: *I love my sister.*

Melissa's at the airport in the next picture.

They set me up.

I see Latoya and Melissa at the brunch for young stars. Everyone eats while Mrs. Paula, the owner of *Sexy Hope* magazine, talks.

"You were invited because you are successful and work hard to help the community," Mrs. Paula says.

I haven't done anything to help the community.

I ask for the bathroom and start to go to my car until I see Sean Johnson, the finest black man alive. I ask for a picture and he says yes. Melissa volunteers to take it. I tell her and Sean thank you.

I get home and there are no pictures.

I get on LuxuryPosts and there's a picture of Lina kissing Sean on the cheek and there's stories about her sleeping with him.

I go to a Chinese restaurant.

The people in front of me leave, and Lina, Erica, Melissa, Lourdes and another girl take their seats.

"Did you guys see what Shanell posted on her page?" Lina asks and gives her phone to Melissa.

"That's what Natalie's ugly ass gets for being such a bitch," Erica says.

"I hate the way she looks," Melissa says. "I hate her face. It doesn't go with her body. I can't believe she has a crush on me." The whole table spits out their water. "She is not my type," Melissa says. "If she thinks I would let her taste me, she's lost her damn mind."

Amber's here. Melissa gives her a kiss on the cheek. Lina captures the moment.

"Look at all these damn pictures this girl has of you in her house," Amber says.

Amber broke the fucking lock to my room and left my door open. "Yea that's right you ugly bitch," Amber says looking at me. "I heard what you said about me so fuck your room. The only annoying tramp is you."

"No," I say. "That's your crew."

"Stupid bitch better learn not to fuck with my sisters," Lina says.

"I don't know what the fuck you're talking about," I say.
"Shut up hoe," Lina says.

18

I give Grant back his I.D. He left it when him and Allen were at my house.

Lina is here. So is Erica, Melissa, Latoya and some other people. They're in the living room.

"Did you do this on purpose?" I ask Grant.

I follow him to his room.

"They came after you called," Grant says.

"Why didn't you call me?" I ask.

"I wasn't thinking about no bullshit," Grant says. "I'll be right back."

A little girl comes in Grant's room. She smiles at me, then leaves. I head out and a mad woman meets me in the hallway.

"You talking shit about my daughter!?" the mad woman yells.

Lina pushes me to the ground.

Melissa and Erica are kicking and stepping on my stomach.

Lina is punching me.

"She's on her period," Erica says.

My period never caused this much pain. Latoya yanks one of my titties.

Grant gets them off of me. The pain increases when he takes me to the bathroom.

"I had a miscarriage," I say. It was his child.

"Damn. I'm sorry Natalie," Grant says. "You can stay here tonight if you want."

I wake up in Grant's bed with Nurse Shelly wiping my forehead.

I passed out.

They hired an in home nurse instead of calling an ambulance. "You're going to be alright," Nurse Shelly says and leaves.

Grant walks in with the lying ass little girl. The mad woman says I called her daughter ugly.

"I didn't," I say.

"I was lying," the lying ass little girl says.

"I'm so sorry," the mother says.

"I didn't know you were pregnant," Melissa says.

"None of us did," Lina says.

"Can someone please tell me what's wrong?" I ask.

"My sisters heard what you said about them," Lina says.

"I never said anything bad about anyone in your family," I say.

"Lynzey and Lesley heard you call them tramps," Melissa says.

"I never said that," I say.

Lina puts Lynzey on speaker.

"Her friend was upset I didn't sign her autograph so she started talking about what I was wearing," Lynzey says. "She called us home wreckers and I couldn't handle another person spreading that lie. They said I was the odd ball in our house and adopted."

"What did Natalie say?" Lina asks.

"I didn't say Natalie said anything," Lynzey says.

Melissa sits next to me.

"You told me she started the conversation," Lina says.

"I said it was her friends," Lynzey says. "I didn't know their names. Natalie's the only person I knew. She wasn't at the table when they were talking about me."

"Why didn't you say something sooner? You saw how we were acting," Lina says.

"I thought you guys just didn't like her," Lynzey says. "I didn't know it was because of me. I didn't tell you she did anything to me. And as far as her friends, you don't have to hate anyone because I do so I didn't care that you were with them."

Melissa is wiping my tears.

"Marty, Marissa and Chasity," I say. "The people you guys are smiling in pictures with and promoting to the world are the ones responsible for your sister trying to kill herself. They were the ones at the table. Your sister didn't take a picture with Marissa and Marissa doesn't take rejection well."

"I would like to apologize," Lina says. "My family has to deal with so many people ripping us apart on a daily basis. When my baby sis tried to kill herself I just reacted the best way I could so she would know I have her back and not try to take her life again."

Lina says they didn't turn Chasity, Marty and Marissa against me, but they did start talking to them just to piss me off.

Melissa says her and Shanell pretended to like me when they heard about Lynzey so I would sleep with Latoya.

It was a setup.

All the way from the tripod.

"They told us about Amber and you keeping your address and the film a secret," Lina says.

"When they started chilling with us and realized the girls hated you they started acting the same way," Grant says.

Melissa calls Chasity.

"When you and your friends were out that night Lynzey and Lesley were at the restaurant, was Natalie calling them tramps and home wreckers, and saying she would spread lies about who their parents were?" Melissa asks.

"No. That was us," Chasity says. "We didn't even know they heard us."

Melissa hangs up in her face.

"I'm sorry for everything lovie," Melissa says. "I never really believed anything Amber told me about you."

"I don't like her," I say. "She overheard what I said and when I got drunk and went to sleep she messed up my house. She saw my room with all your paintings and started making up lies."

"Whatever you want, anything you need, just ask," Erica says.

"I owe you big time," Melissa whispers in my ear. She kisses my forehead.

The mad woman's beating her little girl's ass.

What a present surprise.

19

I'm in my office.

It starts with a desk, computer and printer.

It ends with a picture of Marty, Chasity, Marissa, Melissa, Latoya, Shanell, Erica, Lina, Amber and Lourdes, and every picture and comment they disrespected me in on it, TVs playing the collages of the videos they disrespected me in, and an Operation Revenge sign on the door.

I find gossip on the girls and write notes.

20

PRESTON WILKINS

Lina Mendez is jealous of Lourdes and the only one in the family that can't model. She wishes Lourdes was dead so that the fame could be spread evenly amongst her family. She sleeps with people's boyfriends and husbands when she is upset with them. All those years being compared to the flawless Lourdes fucked up her self-esteem. She is not tough like she puts herself out there to be.

I put ugly paparazzi shots of Lina in cages with animals and her head on animals that are shitting.

I take her modelling photos and put the captions:

This bitch is not a natural.

Misfit.

I need modelling tips.

Help, my face is broken.

I put a picture of Lina at the top saying:

I am not a model.

Lourdes is at the bottom saying:

Duh.

I have Lourdes lying in a casket and Lina smiling over it saying:

Bye bitch. It's my time to shine.

I surround Lina's picture with men she's rumored to have slept with. Sean is one. Grant is two. The caption reads:

Don't fuck with me bitches or I'll fuck with your man.

The chorus to my rap song goes:

Fuck that bitch Lina with her hoeing ass.
She done had every disease I learned about in health class.
She's one ugly ass heifer and she needs to go.
Lorena made a mistake popping her out her coochie hole.
That bitch is fake and phony and she's mean as hell,
I can't believe they just don't toss her in a prison cell.
I know I sound like a mean ass fucking bitch,
but believe me when I say that bitch deserves it.

COMMENTS

That bitch Lina is a hoe. Everyone knows she fucked half the damn rappers in the game.
She's the ugly one in the family.
Knowing Lina she probably did something to piss Preston off.
The Mendez girls think they're the best people walking the Earth. They think they're God's gift to the world.
Finally a song reading that bitch correctly.

Damn. My posts about Lina are taken down.

21

PRESTON WILKINS

Lourdes Mendez thinks she's too good for her own family. She sleeps with industry executives to keep her family relevant. She hates being around kids. They annoy her. She doesn't want any kids because she doesn't want to feed them, change their diapers or clean up after them. She hates walking around with Lina because Lina is the worst looking one in the family.

I pay people to make videos burning Lourdes face on cardboard while saying *fuck the world.* While her face is burning they do a dance and toss her head in a lake.

Some people add dialogue:

Drown away Ms. Mendez.
The world's a better place.
Row, row, row away.
Fuck the Mendez's.

Some people burned the whole Mendez family.

Someone sung:

Oh she's leaving, on that water down the lake.

I post pictures with Lourdes chest out and paste them next to men in nice suits.

The captions read:

You look like you have money.
Take me home.
See something you like?
I can put you inside of me if you put money inside my account.

I put photos of children next to Lourdes throwing up while she looks at them.

I take pictures of Lourdes out with Lina and caption them:

Walk further behind me.

People can see you.

You're going to make me lose money.

I have Lourdes sitting on the porch and her family working the cotton fields with the caption reading:

I'm too good for this family.

I make most of the money now it's time for you bitches to make me some.

COMMENTS

I'm glad someone finally did it.
This is sad.
It's not that serious.
Their family is whack.

22

PRESTON WILKINS
I am Not a Mother

FADE IN.

INT. MELISSA'S HOUSE. NIGHT.

NICK BROWN wants to go to work with his mom, MELISSA BROWN, and they get a visit from a SOCIAL WORKER.

Little Nick: Mom can I go with you?
Melissa: No. I'm going to work.
Someone knocks on the door. Melissa looks through the peephole.
Melissa: Go in the room.
Little Nick: Okay Mom.
Melissa. Can I help you?
Social Worker: Yes. May I come in?
Melissa: I'm on my way to work.
Social Worker: This will only take a few minutes.
Melissa steps outside and shuts her door.
Social Worker: We've been getting complaints that a child is crying for help every night and I just wanted to make sure your son was okay.
Melissa looks angry.
Melissa: No one here is being hurt. I don't have any kids and no one brings any over.
Social Worker: Can I use your bathroom?
Melissa: No.
Melissa locks the door.

The social worker goes back and knocks on Melissa's door.
Nick looks through the peephole.
The social worker sees his shadow under the door.
Nick goes to sleep in his room.
The social worker calls the police.
Social Worker: A child's being abused.
A locksmith opens the door.
Nick is hiding in the dryer.
Officer: Where is your mother?
Little Nick: I got two moms.
Latoya and Melissa do a paternity test and the baby is Melissa's.
The story hits the news and people attack Melissa.

FADE OUT.

Preston does a video and in the last scene goes to Melissa's house. The social worker walks in and he says *daddy's home.*

COMPETITION

Whoever portrays where they think Melissa hides her son when she doesn't want to be seen with him the best wins $200. The last line must be: Mommy can I come out now?

Melissa walks around with a child she claims is not hers but her oldest sister's. She can-not act. She has a nasty attitude and is fake. She's in a relationship with Amber. She is using Lina for publicity. It's really Lourdes she wants to be friends with.

COMMENTS

We want more episodes.
The baby is hers.

Tori calls. "Happy 28th Birthday girl! How you feel?"
"Hung over," I say. "And I'm still drinking."

23

PRESTON WILKINS

I post Erica's mugshot.

The summary reads as follows: *Erica is friends with Lina and Melissa and they didn't want to help her pay her taxes. They'd rather her get a mugshot than give her money. Erica doesn't get that they don't want her around. And I thought Erica was an actress. How come she couldn't afford to pay her taxes?*

COMMENTS

This is so old. Can people let me move on with my life? Who likes to keep thinking about the bad shit that's happened in the past? Fuck Preston.

It's Erica.

I post a picture of Lina dragging Erica on a leash.

24

PRESTON WILKINS

Shanell Gear is a crackhead and she has chlamydia. Vaginal cream fell out her purse.

I have girls that look like Shanell act like they're on crack and drop vaginal cream. They pick it up, look at the cameras then run.

I have people sing Shanell's songs like they're on crack.

I'm watching Shanell's sex tape.

I have people make parodies of it.

COMMENTS

Shanell could get it if I didn't think she really had every STD known to man.
Ya'll stupid if ya'll still want to hit that.
That bitch could still get it. She so damn sexy. The cream wasn't for her it was for her friend.

▲

I put on Preston's body and meet a rapper named Markus at a studio. I thank him and he says, "My kids got to eat. I don't give a fuck about nobody's Lina."

When Markus leaves Vicky and Judith walk in. They're going to cover Shanell's songs. Better than she can.

When my crew leaves, I take off my disguise and chill in the studio.

Shanell walks in.

"The girls told you I was sorry right?" Shanell asks.

"I forgive you," I say.

"Can I try some?" Shanell asks. I give her some shrimp fried rice. "So what's been going on with you?" she asks.

"I'm just playing around with this equipment," I say.

She takes pictures with me. She kisses my cheek and intertwines her arm with mine.

When we get outside there's camera's everywhere.

Shanell won't answer the paparazzi's questions:

Do you have chlamydia?

Why does Preston hate you?

What are you going to do to get him back?

When I get home I see that the behind the scenes footage of Vicky and Judith covering Shanell's songs were removed.

Shanell posted a picture of Preston's head on a black man's body. The comment under the picture says:

They always wanted to be us.

25

PRESTON WILKINS

Chasity McClinton is nosy and talks too much. She can't remember to run errands so how can she be a pediatrician?

I hire a spy. His names Chester. He gives me a flashdrive of Chasity eating the hell out of a woman and five pictures of her kissing different women.

I upload it to a porn site.

I create pictures of Chasity with kids frowning and the word pediatrician on a stop sign crossed out; and pictures of her with a long nose, duct tape over her lips, and a kid using his finger to tell her to shut up.

I upload the five pictures with five different women kissing her.

PRESTON WILKINS

Marissa is stupid as shit. She won't leave a man she knows is cheating on her.

The Light Way

Synopsis:

Marissa enjoys her date until a light skinned woman walks up and takes her man's attention. Marissa looks at the woman with disgust from head to toe. Her boyfriend looks at the light lady then at Marissa and shoots Marissa in the head. Marissa comes back to life and says, "I knew you would leave me when you saw someone lighter." Then her man shoots her again and walks off with the light lady.

I record the scene.

COMMENTS

*Light skin does not automatically make someone beautiful.
People need to stop dividing black people.
We are all beautiful no matter what shapes and sizes.
Any woman can get this dick.
Preston needs his ass beat for this shit.
Why would someone want to depict a scene like this?*

I post the pictures Chester took of Marissa's boyfriend kissing other women and squeezing their asses.

The title reads:

*This Handsome Young Man Should Be a Model.
Different Days, Different Girls.*

The summary reads:

This nice looking man is dating Marissa Clay. Marissa knows he is cheating, and like so many other women, she just don't care. Why can't I find any pictures of him and Marissa together?

COMMENTS

*This bitch gives dark skinned sisters a bad name.
Man it's sad that people with no self-esteem will settle for a trifling man.
Preston it's not a doubt in my mind that bitch didn't know her man was cheating.*

Marissa is a dumb broad.
Hope the bitch at least gets a checkup.

Marissa's comments on LuxuryPosts:
Get out of the relationship.
You stupid and a terrible example.
Never reproduce.
She should know her man would leave her for a light bitch.
Can I take you on a date?
She can do better.
No. Preston can do better and add more videos.

Marissa's response: *I want everyone to know I am no longer dating Ryan. I honestly had no idea what he was doing behind my back. I am not uncomfortable in my skin. I love being a dark skinned woman. I love my heritage, race, and culture. If I wanted to be lighter I could've taken the necessary steps to do so. Please do not judge me on some stupid storyline that this boy came up with. And Preston, you are one fucked up person. I didn't do anything to you. I don't even know you. Why do I have your attention?*

I respond: *You have my attention because I hate women who don't love the way God made them.*

Marissa responds: *I love the way I was made, I just hate that ugly heart of yours.*

.

Me and Tori are drinking margaritas in my backyard.

26

Me, Spencer and George take pictures on the red carpet and sign autographs at the *Fools Back Out* premiere.

I do an interview and have to end it with, "Hi. I'm Natalie McIntyre and you're watching Money Trill TV."

"Why didn't you tell me you were in a movie?" my mom asks.

"I didn't think it was a big deal," I say.

"You're about to be in theaters and you didn't think it was a big deal?" Mom asks.

"Sorry," I say. "I've been so busy I forgot I didn't tell you."

George calls and says he has me set to go on the Darla Penn Network.

27

"How did you prepare to play Melody in *Fools Back Out*?" Ms. Darla asks.

"I practiced my lines in the mirror," I say. "If I can't believe my own emotions then I can't expect anyone else to."

"What was it like working with George?" Ms. Darla asks. I say it was great and I learned a lot from him.

"Like what?" Ms. Darla asks. I say to be patient when it comes to mistakes.

"Are you the type that doesn't add to your circle once the fame comes because you're not sure who's using you for your success?" Ms. Darla asks.

"No," I say.

Ms. Darla asks me about my costars, how I got selected to do the project, and how my life has changed since I've been on the big screen.

I say nothing but good things.

"I hope to see you again," Ms. Darla says.

I have a house party.

I take pictures and record videos of everyone drinking, dancing, smoking, and eating and post them on LuxuryPosts.

When everyone leaves, I relax in my Operation Revenge room.

28

I'm at a pizzeria. I eat one slice then walk. I hold my heart tight and fall to the ground. The pizzeria workers rush to me. The ambulance pulls up.

"Sir are you okay?" the paramedic asks.

I'm at another premiere for *Fools Back Out*.

Spencer's sitting next to me. "I wanted to apologize to you for what happened," he says.

I ask Ebony for the manager.

"He's not here," Ebony says. "Neither is the tape. After you left Lourdes and Lorena came back and gave him money. Lourdes picked him up after he got off too. I wish I could get it for you. That was some fucked up shit."

"I thought you liked Lourdes," I say.

"I did," Ebony says. "But fuck her. She don't get a pass to act like a bitch because she's famous."

"This the cutest white boy I ever seen," Tori says.

"Preston is nice," I say taking off my mask.

29

I'm on a movie set.

Lucas Mendez is here.

I go in the bathroom and Lucas is waiting by the door when I get out the stall. He tells me I'm doing good and asks, "Do you have a girl somewhere?" I say no. "You want to come by tonight?" he asks. I follow him to his condo.

I trip over a baby bottle. "So what's stressing you out?" Lucas asks.

"Family," I say. "It takes a lot for me to get over the shit they do to me." I pick up one of his baby bottles. "So this is what makes a baby stop crying."

"Would you like me to make you feel better?" Lucas asks.

We kiss.

I grip his dick and suck it. I have my phone in my other hand. "Say my name," I say.

"Preston!" Lucas yells.

I pull around the corner.

Good.

I got his face.

30

"How are you Preston?" Ms. Darla asks.

"Good," I say. "You look beautiful."

"Thank you," Ms. Darla says. "You have really just taken the world by storm. You're in magazines and modelling. How come the world is just now learning who PRESTON WILKINS is?"

"I've always been a home body," I say. "I don't like to leave the house a lot."

"So you don't like to go out and socialize often?" Ms. Darla asks.

"No," I say. "Even in school I always kept to myself. My mom was the same way growing up."

"How is mom and dad?" Ms. Darla asks.

"They died," I say.

"Okay now that I've completely changed the atmosphere," Ms. Darla says.

"Ms. Darla it's all good," I say.

"When did you decide you wanted to be an actor?" Ms. Darla asks.

"I was watching my friend on a movie set and she inspired me to give it a shot," I say.

"She," Ms. Darla says.

"Yes, she," I say.

"Now the other day you passed out," Ms. Darla says. "Can you tell us what happened?"

"At first I was going to keep this to myself because the people that broke me down are so big in the entertainment world. I didn't want them to think I was bringing it up for publicity, but I don't care anymore. I was out eating and Lina,

Erica and Melissa were behind me."

"You are talking about the famous trio with Lina Mendez right?" Ms. Darla asks. "The trio everyone is in love with and you said you don't want to talk about your account, right?"

"Yes," I say. "They were talking bad about the disabled. They said handicap people are disgusting to be around. They could never be friends with them. When my parents were paralyzed, everyone left. I was thinking about them when they were saying that shit. The driver that hit my parents is going to be out in fifteen years. I don't get my parents back."

We finish the interview talking about all the projects Preston's worked on.

Ms. Darla gives me a tight hug, a coffee mug and a copy of her biography.

I'm watching the news. The Mendez crew is saying Preston's a liar.

All of them except Lucas.

Lina says: *No one in my family has ever said anything disrespectful about anyone disabled.*

Lorena says: *My family is not like that. We would never say any of those things.*

Lourdes says: *I don't know him.*

Lana, the oldest Mendez says: *I wish people would just leave us alone.*

Lynzey says: *He's nothing but a liar.*

Lesley says: *He just wants more fame.*

Lorena says: *Lawsuits and gag orders have been filed.*

Me and Tori have dinner.

31

I guest star on TV shows, make dance videos, and do a book signing for *Get In, Ghetto Out*. I take pictures with my fans and shoot videos rapping songs.

As myself.

Melissa and Latoya are waving to me on the set of The Yoop's House. My costar is not here and I find out Melissa is taking her place.

I'm in my Operation Revenge room looking at my wall posts and Chasity calls. She wants me to go skating with her, Marty and Marissa.

Chasity's by the lockers. She asks me if I've been alright and I say yes and, "What you been up to?"

"Shit," Chasity says. "Just trying to keep my head above water."

"Marty still struggling in them skates I see," I say.

"Hell yea," Chasity says. "I miss you."

"I miss you too," I say. "Small shit gets taken to new heights all the time. It's over. We good."

Her little cousin skates over eating cake. "Hi," Jamia says. I say hi and tell her I didn't know it was her birthday.

"I'm surprised you came," Marissa says.

"Look," I say. "I fucked up with ya'll too. We're even. I'm done with that shit. Let's skate."

32

I'm at the store trying on clothes. I'm hosting *Model's Run It* again and need something to wear.

I can't find my purse.

"It's over there by the shorts," Lesley says.

One of my models can't make it to the show so I ask Lesley if she can fill in. I give her the information and she says yes.

Lynzey comes out the dressing room and says she'll do the show too.

I text Tori:

Natalie: Have fill ins ready.

33

Lynzey chases behind Lesley who runs in the bathroom.

"She's upset our family can't make it," Lynzey says.

"Dad, get here now!" Lesley yells. She hangs up on him and calls Lina. "Please try to come."

Lynzey is the only one here.

My crew opens the show dancing.

We kill it.

The models, projectors, music, lighting, effects, fog and wind machines are all on point.

The Mendez family made it.

After the show, Lina congratulates me on putting it together and says, "I loved you on *Do More Get More*." I say thanks.

I invite her crew to my house for dinner and drinks and she says they'll be there.

♥

I'm spinning around in my chair in my Operation Revenge room when Lina, Erica, and Melissa get to my house.

We smoke and talk about fame and friends.

"Once you get big, you might as well say fuck your clique," Lina says. "Some will be jealous and some will try and ruin you."

"That's right," Melissa says. "Don't be quick to make no friends. They turn on you fast when you get money."

"People will leave they families for money," Erica says.

"I stay true to myself," I say.

"That's good," Melissa says. "Always remember saying yes to

the wrong person can ruin your life."

We're passing the blunt and listening to music.

When I come out the bathroom, Melissa isn't in the room.

I find her in the room with all my paintings of her.

She's lying in the bed that has sheets of her face on it. Her movies are playing and so are slideshows of her pictures.

The room is now complete.

Melissa sees a picture I haven't finished of her and tells me to finish it.

"My sister wants to know if she can still get that favor you owe her?" Melissa asks.

"I did my part," I say.

"Look at me," she says. She uncrosses her legs and adjusts her body. "I was hoping you would reconsider."

When I finish, everyone goes to the backyard.

Still smoking.

"Have you ever had to sleep with anyone for a role?" Lina asks. Erica says yes. "I was talking to Melissa," Lina says.

"The bigger you get the more hell you have to deal with," Melissa says.

"What does that mean?" Lina asks.

"Yes," Erica says and asks Lina what's wrong.

"I'm sick of that boy," Lina says. "My family hasn't done anything to him."

"Fuck Preston," Erica says. "He'll get his."

"I'm going to have Lucas fuck him up," Lina says. "I don't care if it's the red carpet or the streets. I want to ruin him. I want his career to be over."

34

I buzz Latoya, Melissa and their friend Peter in.

I take pictures of Melissa inside and outside with different clothes and backgrounds.

Latoya and Peter go to the car.

Melissa calls me in the bathroom. "Can you tie this in the back?" she asks. I tie the strings to her bikini top. She sits me down, stands over me and asks me to hold the bottom strings together on one side while she ties the other.

Her cats in my face.

She turns around and ties the other side.

Her ass is in my face.

We get drinks and go by the pool with Peter and Latoya.

I turn music on in my backhouse. Melissa comes in.

"Why do you have this bed in here?" Melissa asks.

"You never know when you won't make it to your room," I say. Melissa sips from my straw.

"What ya'll doing in there?" Peter yells.

"Minding our business," Melissa says.

She lies next to me on the bed.

Peter and Latoya come in and we smoke another blunt before they head out.

Peter's car won't start.

"Since I'm here you might as well let me make this night for you," Melissa says. We go to my room and have sex.

I let the pole down from the ceiling and dance around it. We eat each other, smoke and eat snacks.

There's rumors on the blogs about me and Melissa fucking. She denies them and sends me a text:

Melissa: ;)

The news is interviewing people that worked with Preston. They can't find him.

35

"Started to think you ain't like dick no more," Allen says.

"I just want some company," I say. He's rubbing my thighs. I tell him to stop. I can smell the alcohol on his breath. "Not today Allen." He pushes me on the table. He's trying to rape me. "Stop!" I scream. I hit him on the head with a vase and he throws me on the floor.

Someone's beating on the door.

It's Grant.

He punches the fuck out of Allen and Allen trips over his pants.

He falls and Grant steps on his dick.

Allen's screaming. He gets a gun out his truck and I shut the front door. "Scary ass nigga!" Allen yells.

My bodyguard beat the fuck out of my boxing trainer.

It's a good thing Grant needed to pick up his check.

I get in the shower. Grant washes me off.

"Do you want me to stay?" he asks.

"I'm fine," I say. I grab his check off my nightstand. "Here."

Sky and Jamie don't answer so I call Melissa.

I buzz her in. She holds me tight.

"Amber denied everything," Melissa says. "She said she really was hacked. Then she forgot to hang up before she told her boy she was lying to me."

"When something's on the internet it's there forever," I say. "Time won't even work."

"So tell me what I need to do?" Melissa asks.

"What?" I ask.

"You keep bringing that shit up," Melissa says.

"I'm not bringing shit up," I say.

"I didn't mean none of that shit I said," Melissa says. "Lina couldn't sleep that night we left Grant's. She was up all night trying to figure out how to make it up to you."

"I feel better," I say. "I didn't call you over here because of none of that. Stupid ass Allen pissed me the fuck off."

"Girl fuck these men," Melissa says. "Preston still making videos about me and my son and he never lets people know where the fuck he gone be in advance. I wish my baby daddy was out. He'd kill that bastard."

"Your baby daddy?" I ask.

"Don't say nothing. If you want to know if I'm ashamed that I had a child by a killer then yes I am, but he's about our damn son. Preston's not even thinking about my son being in school one day."

She's rolling a blunt.

Now driving. We pull up to a house I never been to.

"Surprise!" everyone screams.

Melissa, Erica and Lina threw me an *I'm Sorry* party.

They went all out with food, drinks and decorations.

Erica and her sister Esther give me a hug.

"Do whatever you want girl," Melissa says. I turn around and my lips are forced against Sean Johnson's. Melissa, Lina and Erica are taking pictures.

Me and Sean dance and Lorena bumps into me.

She's drunk.

While I'm making my plate Lucas introduces himself and his wife, Rachael, to me. He tells her he'll be back when two men walk by.

Lynzey and Lesley pull me on the dance floor and Lina, Melissa, Erica and Esther follow us.

Melissa comes back to my house and we get comfortable

under covers. "So how long have you had a crush on me?" Melissa asks.

"What makes you think I have a crush on you?" I ask.

"A lot of women do," she says. I tell her she's conceited.

"Just like everybody likes me to be," she says.

Melissa turns on the news and I fall to the floor.

Headline:

Chasity Kelley overdosed on pills.

The reporter says: *"Her family says she couldn't handle being outted to the world. They say her mother who is a preacher at Salem Christ Church was embarrassed by the footage and lashed out at Chasity a few times. Family and friends of Chasity think her mother played a huge part in her overdosing and lying in a tub full of water. By the time her ten year old sister found her, it was too late."*

Melissa holds me tight.

Chasity is gone.

The weekend of the funeral, I see Marty and Marissa.

They catch up to me while I'm walking to my car. Marty gives me a hug. "Stay safe," she says.

"You too," I say.

I post the funeral brochure on Preston's website.

COMMENTS

Preston is wrong.
He needs to be in prison.
Heartless mutha fucka.

    My mom's calling.
    "You doing alright baby?" she asks. I say no. "No one had to out her. Not like that."
    I tell my mom I need to take a nap and pour myself a drink.
    Tori's at the door.
    I'm tipsy. I flop on the couch and she pours herself a drink.
    I tell Tori about Lucas and Rachael.
    "Why you ain't invite me to the party?" Tori asks.
    "Girl I didn't know where we was going," I say.
    Me and Tori read Lina's LuxuryPosts status: *Preston is ignorant. I haven't done anything to him. I don't deserve this shit. I don't know what his problem is.*
    Melissa reposts all of Lina's statuses and says: *Preston, you're fucked up. Talking about my son is not okay. He has done nothing to you.*
    I repost Lina's statuses and comment: *Don't worry about it girl. God is watching. He will take care of that evil bastard.*

    I'm driving home from the store.
    The song I wrote about Lina is playing.
    I call Markus. "You on the radio," I say.
    "I know," Markus says. "And don't trip. My dad is a lawyer."

36

I release the footage of Preston giving Lucas head on a porn site.

It's removed after a minute.

Lucas denies that it's him.

PRESTON WILKINS

Lucas is gay. Fans, family and friends, it is in fact Lucas in the video with me. I recorded the video and sent it to him. I did not post it so that only leaves one person. I can't believe he's acting like he's not the one that uploaded the video to the porn site. I didn't know he was married at the time. I guess this was his way of showing his wife he no longer wanted to be with her. I'm very upset I am involved in this. I want to take this time to apologize to his wife, any kids he may have, and anyone else I may have hurt. This is one of many lessons I will learn on this journey called life.

I tell everyone Preston got a new phone.

COMMENTS

Man Preston don't know what he's doing.
Preston come my way.
I can't believe they're gay.
I never would think they were gay.
Why the hell would they want this shit on the internet?

Tori sends me a picture she made of Lucas giving Preston head with the caption reading: *Payback Bitch.*

I take a headshot of Preston and caption it: *Hi.*
Tori texts me:

Tori: Lina went to the hospital and got her fat switched in different places.

I text Tori:

Natalie: Damn. Lol.

I text Lina.

Natalie: Mama don't stress over that shit. It comes with being famous. This too shall pass.

PRESTON WILKINS

COMMENTS

Lina will always be the odd ball.
I don't think she looks bad.
She didn't need the surgery.
I thought she was strong.
What message is she giving young girls?

Lina texts me:

Lina: Come out to eat with us. I'll pick you up.

I'm riding with her, Erica and Melissa in the car she tried to run me over with.
I'm mad they're not angry enough to stay home.
Cameras blind us the entire walk into the restaurant.
We sit with three other people.
I don't know who they are.
Everyone orders a margarita.
Lina orders two shots.

The waitress hands her one and she throws it back.

The waitress hands her the second one and she downs that too, then drinks her margarita.

Melissa takes Lina's keys and puts them in her purse.

The three girl's names are Kaylee, Amelia and Elena.

We talk about our projects and boyfriends until the food arrives.

The smell of someone's food is making my stomach act up.

Elena asks if I'm okay. I tell her I feel like I'm about to throw up.

I hold my stomach the whole walk to the bathroom and crouch down by the wall.

Melissa checks on me. "Are you okay lovie?" she asks. I tell her no.

The waitress hands Lina some crackers. "Here. Eat these," Lina says. "They'll help."

I say thank you and after eating that shit I feel better.

Amelia is bucking her head and rolling her eyes at someone behind me. "Wasup?" I ask her.

"This bitch keeps rolling her eyes at me," Amelia says. "She thinks I'm trying to look at her man. Fucking dumb bitch. I can barely see his ass. Can I be checking for the man that just walked by? I fucking can't stand bitches."

"Girl welcome to the club," Melissa says. "A lot of women get insecure when they man see me. Some people don't invite me over when they man home."

As time goes by Lina starts looking sadder and sadder.

"What's wrong?" I ask.

She's crying.

"Lina what's wrong baby?" Elena asks.

"I just wish my mom didn't have to stress trying to figure out why all this shit is happening," Lina cries.

Erica hugs her.

"Lucas isn't doing anything but smoking, drinking and eating," Lina cries. She can't get herself together so we call it a night.

A man bumps into me on our way out and Lina pushes him to the floor.

It's official.

I am one of them now.

Lina's throwing up by the car.

Melissa turns on the radio. Dalton's song about me is on. Melissa turns the station.

"Natalie I'm really sorry about the song," Lina cries. "Me and Dalton have been telling everyone to stop playing it and they won't."

"Once it's out there it's out there," I say. "Even if it wasn't on the radio, people are still reading it on the internet. Some got it on CDs. It will exist forever."

37

PRESTON WILKINS

Shanell Gear made a gay joke about me. She said I was more appealing when she thought I was straight. She said she was uncomfortable with me around her. I hate how she looks at me. It's because of people like her that people like Chasity Kelley overdose. The pain homophobes give to gay people is unbearable. Sometimes I feel like death is better.

COMMENTS

Fuck her Preston. Shanell has no reason to hate because we all know she's bisexual.
Keep your head up Preston.
Don't check out because of that bitch Preston.

Shanell gets on LuxuryPosts: PRESTON WILKINS *is something else. I've never met him. I love the gay community.*

She posts a picture with two of her male fans that are wearing heels and reposts Lina's status: *We all seem to be victims of internet bullying* and Melissa's: *Fuck you Preston.*

I'm watching the news. Shanell's getting mad at a man that asked her if she really hated the gay community. "Shut the fuck up," Shanell says.

38

PRESTON WILKINS

I was hacked.

39

Me and Tori are decorating my house.

Halloween is coming up.

"Now let's see if they asses believe he was hacked," Tori says.

"Stupid ass bitches," I say. "This they own prescription."

"And I enjoy watching them under the influence," Tori says. "And reading all the shit people saying."

She pops some popcorn and we watch *I am Not a Mother*.

"Lucas still denying that damn sex tape," I say. "I'm glad Rachael divorced his ass."

"Now he walking around with two girls every other day," Tori says.

"Yep," I say. "And Lorena got cameras following them."

"You know she good at damage control," Tori says.

"They show losing ratings," I say. "This the last season."

"Nobody watched that shit," Tori says. "Fuck them. It's a new day in age. I'm tired of dumb ass bitches fucking with people."

"And over the stupidest shit," I say.

Me and Tori hang lights in the backyard and lay on my beach chairs and stare at the sky.

"You ever wish you could be a star for a night?" Tori asks.

"I've been a star for a while," I say.

"You know what I mean," Tori says. "You ever wish you could see the world from a star's perspective?"

"No," I say. "I'm scared of heights."

"I wish I was high enough to see most of the world," Tori says.

"You should be an astronaut," I say.

"That or a damn pilot," she says.

"Well I can't get you as high as that but I can get some blunts," I say.

We go in my Operation Revenge room and light three candles.

We take a shot and smoke.

I'm at Tori's Halloween party.

I'm a witch.

"So this how you feeling?" Tori asks.

"It is," I say. "You look cute." She's a princess.

"These are my people," Tori says. "Don't be shy."

40

"Lorena's going on the Darla Penn Show," Tori says. We make a big dinner and have our drinks and blunts ready.

"Why would Preston lie and say Lina talks bad about disabled people?" Ms. Darla asks.

"We don't know why he's doing this to our family," Lorena says. "None of my kids have met him. We've tried contacting him but no one can reach him."

"It puzzles me that he's trying to make it further in his career and he would lie on the biggest reality family there is," Ms. Darla says. "So everything he said was a lie?"

"Yes," Lorena says. "He made a name for himself and disappeared."

"What else do you want to tell the audience about your family?" Ms. Darla asks.

"My family is not a bad family," Lorena says. "We work hard every day. We're humble. We would never say or do anything to hurt anyone. That's not who we are."

"Lying bitch," I say.

"We've filed a police report," Lorena says. "My daughter will not be the next Chasity Kelley."

"What upsets you the most when it comes to the media and your children?" Ms. Darla asks.

Lorena's crying. "I hate when people compare them and talk about the way they look," she says. "They are all beautiful. I know it may not seem like it, but it rips them a part."

I turn off the TV and Tori gives me a high five and says, "You got they ass's girl."

41

My mom, Nathan, Natonya and her kids are eating at my house.

I turn the AC off and Denise and Rhea volunteer to get me a sweater. "Don't touch nothing," I say while they run up the stairs. "Just grab any sweater."

It's been five minutes and the girls haven't came back down.

"TT you were Preston for Halloween?" Denise asks when I get to my room.

"Yes," I say. "Let's go."

Natonya's at the door. "Girls go downstairs," she says and shuts the door behind her kids. "So you're PRESTON WILKINS."

"I was him for Halloween," I say.

"I saw your witch costume on LuxuryPosts," Natonya says.

"I went to more than one party," I say.

"Oh you went to more than one party?" Natonya asks. "Shit. You could've gotten me a costume and I could've helped you get them bitches back."

"TT I like your house," Denise says.

"Go back downstairs," Natonya says.

"I want to spend the night," Denise says and shuts the door.

Denise and Rhea fall asleep in the theater and Natonya and Mom sleep in the bed with me.

42

PRESTON WILKINS

WILL NATALIE JUST DIE?

Hey ya'll know Natalie McIntyre, that actress from the film Fools Back Out? Remember when Shanell said she has threesomes? Have you seen the pictures Melissa, Erica and Lina posted of that bitch? She does resemble them cheetahs. Do cheetahs have threesomes?

I collage a picture of me and two men in bed.

I repost the photos Melissa, Erica, and Lina posted of me and animals.

I put a link to Dalton's song and comment: *The song is dope. If you haven't heard it you're missing out.*

I let Tori in.

We countdown to the new year in my Operation Revenge room.

We take a shot.

I respond to my post: *I can't believe I'm starting the New Year with someone attacking me. Preston, you are not going to ruin my year. I have a lot I am going to accomplish. The devil never stops working.*

"Good shit," Tori says. "Using that shit them bitches fucked you over with to make them look for answers elsewhere is pure genius girl."

PRESTON WILKINS

COMMENTS

That bitch looks like she likes two dicks in her at once.
Preston would you go in her?
Natalie is a tramp.
Shanell has no reason to lie on Natalie.
Natalie must've really pissed Shanell off.
This is what Natalie gets.
She needs to be exposed so she never fucks with the Stupendous Shanell again.

43

I'm at Melissa's house with Lina, Lourdes, Erica, Latoya, Marty, Marissa, Shanell, Lana and Esther.

"Alright," Melissa says. "Now that everyone's here, let's put our heads together and try to put an end to this shit. Has anyone here ever met Preston?" Everyone says no. "Does anyone know someone that he knows or someone you think he might know?" Everyone says no. "So he's fucking with all of us and none of us knows why?"

"I'm so sick of this shit," Lina says.

"What the fuck is his problem?" Erica asks. "It's not a coincidence we're the only people he hates."

"I mean come on," Lana says. "He pursues acting for a while, makes himself known, then disappears. He planned this. You guys need to think long and hard. Who have you pissed off in the past months? Who hates you? Who's he working for?"

"The only person I don't talk to anymore is Amber," Melissa says. "After I overheard her say she lied about everything with Natalie I was done with her."

"You guys think Amber is behind all this?" Marty asks.

"It would make sense," I say. "Maybe she knows Preston and told him to do this shit."

"He hasn't said anything about Marty," Marissa says.

"And no I'm not behind none of this shit," Marty says.

"Does anyone still have Amber's number?" Lina asks.

Marty does.

"Ask her if she knows Preston," Latoya says.

"Wasup?" Amber asks.

"Do you know PRESTON WILKINS?" Marty asks.

"Whose fucking business is that?" Amber asks.

"Marissa can't deal with the shit he saying about her and I want to figure out what the problem is so she don't take her life like Chasity," Marty says. "It's Preston I want. Not you."

"I've never met him," Amber says.

"So if it's not her, then who?" Latoya asks.

"She could be lying," I say. "If that's her friend she not gone tell us where he's at."

"I never thought about taking a life until this shit," Lina says.

"Me too," I say.

Everyone looks at me.

"You mean that?" Lina asks.

"I do," I say "I'm so damn mad, I could kidnap his ass, lock him in the basement, torture him for every bad thing he's said about me, then put him in the trunk and drive him into a lake. My mother hasn't been able to sleep since he started fucking with me. She thinks I'll kill myself just like Chasity."

"He can't hide forever," Shanell says. "He'll come out."

"And when he does, we'll get his ass," Lina says.

Everyone leaves except me. I stay with Melissa.

I bring some paintings in and Melissa hands me some nails.

"Are you asking me to hang these somewhere?" I ask.

"Thanks," Melissa says.

I hang them and leave.

I ring the doorbell.

"Can I have something to drink?" I ask.

"You know you not thirsty," Melissa says.

"I am," I say. "Putting those pictures up was hard work."

"You're lucky I still feel bad," she says.

I hear someone crying. Her son comes running to the front room. "Nick what's wrong?" Melissa asks. "Did you have a nightmare again?" He keeps crying. Melissa lies him on the couch.

Nick is staring at me.

I say hi and he waves.

Melissa brings him some crackers and juice. "Eat that and get back in the bed," she says. "How long does it take to drink water?" she asks me.

"Something's making my throat itch," I say.

"I bet there is," she says. "While you try to prolong your visit, do me a favor and watch him while I get in the shower."

Yes. I get to stay longer.

"Was it good?" I ask Nick about the crackers. He says yes and presses the power button on the TV.

"What do you want to watch?" Nick asks.

"Whatever you want to," I say. "How old are you?"

"Four," Nick says.

He turns to a court show.

He goes in the kitchen, comes out with the whole bag of crackers and sits next to me.

He puts the bag in my face.

His eyes are glued to the TV so he doesn't see he's scratching me with the bag.

"No thanks," I say.

He puts it closer to my face with his eyes still glued to the TV. I eat some.

"You watch my mom on TV?" Nick asks. I say yes. "You know Lina?" he asks. I say yes. "She my friend."

Nick pours puzzle pieces on the table and asks me to help him put it together.

"Nick come here!" Melissa shouts. She tells him to grab her shirt off the bed.

Nick's screaming.

He's holding his leg.

"What happened?" I ask.

Melissa's standing by her room door wrapped in a towel.

"I hit my leg on the side of the bed!" Nick screams.

Melissa grabs her shirt.

I pick Nick up and walk around.

"It's okay. I hit my toe on my bed before," I say. "I cried too but it got better the next day." He stops screaming.

He's drenching my shirt with his tears.

He falls asleep and I put him on the couch.

When I turn around Melissa's behind me.

She takes me to her room.

I eat her.

Sweet revenge.

44

The costume designers are on TV saying they built Preston.

"I didn't show them I.D. I gave them a fake name and I paid them cash. They're not going to remember me," Tori says.

Fans are requesting a missing report for Preston.

"I wonder how long it's going to take them to find the ghost of Preston," Tori says.

"If they ever see his ass they better walk the other direction," I say.

45

LuxuryPosts

PRESTON WILKINS

Those hoes just want attention and money. I know my parents are turning in their graves. It hurts that people think I don't have feelings. And fuck that bitch Marty. She has self-esteem issues. She's not comfortable being a dark sister. She gets intimidated every time someone lighter is in the room.

COMMENTS

You are not a human just like Melissa is not a mother.

I post pictures of Marty's body with the devil's head and white sheets.

The Many Disguises of the Enemy.

Satan comes in infinite forms.

Guess who's beneath the head.

This person Satan was disguised as to ruin my life. He used her to befriend me and steal from my house.

It's Marty.

Marty gets on LuxuryPosts: *You are calling me the devil but you are the red neck. I am not evil, and you are the devil.*

46

PRESTON WILKINS

Lovers

I post a photo I created of Amber and Melissa kissing.

Rumor has it that dating a Latino has always been a fantasy of Melissa's. However, it's been said by numerous people that Amber has a disease that can't be cured. They're gay so Melissa has put her mouth on Amber's pussy. Melissa has a nasty attitude. She deserves to have the disease. It will give her something else to talk about.

I post a collage of Lina and Melissa with a zig zag line going down the middle.

The Truth

Melissa uses Lina for publicity. Lina wants to be Lourdes and Lourdes knows it. Has anyone seen any of Erica's movies? Did you know she was an actress before you read this? Erica is a no name without Lina too.

COMMENTS

I never knew she acted.
Wait. Erica's in a film?
I just thought she was Lina's best friend.
I watched one movie she was in and never supported her again.
Preston leave my sister the fuck alone. She's a very successful actress.

I screenshot Esther's post and title it: *LOL.*
The summary reads: *Successful?*

47

This is my friend Tori," I say.

Stefan says hi.

"Damn, I heard about a lot of this," Stefan says.

We're in my Operation Revenge room.

"I asked them what the problem was and none of them wanted to tell me until they made me have a miscarriage," I say.

"Them bitches killed your child?" Tori asks.

"I would not be fucking with nobody that did all that shit to me," Stefan says. "I'd be trying to figure out a way to get they asses back."

Me and Tori look at him.

"Oh so you need me to help you wreck some shit huh?" Stefan asks. "Tell me what to do."

48

Me, Tori and Stefan are eating pizza in front of my house.

"Whose cars we using?" Stefan asks.

"We can use mine if somebody's going to get me another one," Tori says looking at me.

"I will," I say.

"You okay?" Tori asks me. "Don't trip over the miscarriage. I had two."

"I think every woman goes through at least one," Stefan says.

"I'm alright," I say. "I didn't want it anyways. I'm just pissed at how dumb them bitches are."

"All that shit because of a few words someone told them you said and you ain't even say shit," Stefan says. "Let's fuck some shit up."

"I fucking can't stand bitches today," Tori says. "They always feel like somebody's out to get them."

"You need to write a song about all this shit," Stefan says.

"I'll do it if you hop on it," I say.

"I'll hop on it if I can see you in Preston's costume," Stefan says.

We eat the whole box of pizza and still no call from Chester.

"You got some drinks?" Stefan asks.

"You're about to drive," I say. "After we do this I'll hook you up."

"I saw that," Tori says. Stefan winks back at me.

"I'm gone go see my boo tonight anyways," Tori says.

I'm yawning.

"You better be ready for that damn call," Tori says.

I turn on the radio.

Midnight hits and we go inside.

"Ya'll want to call it a night?" I ask.

"No," Stefan says. "Thought you was making me something to eat?"

"You for real still hungry?" I ask.

Stefan nods his head.

"Everything's closed," Tori says.

"Not the pizza place," Stefan says.

My phone rings.

"They left," Chester says. "No one's at the house."

We leave.

Stefan's calling me.

"Why they behind us?" Stefan asks.

Lina and her crew are going back to her house.

Stefan makes the next right with me.

We're parked around the corner from Lina's house.

"Shit I'm hungry," Stefan says.

"Go run in the diner over there," Tori says.

"Can you get it for me?" Stefan asks. "I'll pay you back."

Me and Tori don't say nothing.

"Fuck it," Stefan says. "I'll be back."

"Hurry please and leave the phone on speaker," I say.

Minutes later.

"It's packed in here with a bunch of high school kids and prostitutes," Stefan says.

"What's that noise?" I ask.

"A homeless woman is asking everybody to buy her something," Stefan says. "We all said no."

"Give me some change!" I hear the homeless lady scream.

"I don't have any," Stefan says. "Don't throw no damn chair at me!"

"Just come on Stefan," I say. "I swear I'll make something at the house."

I hear sirens.

Through the phone.

"Five more minutes," the cashier says to Stefan. "Stop throwing food on the floor ma'am!"

"I'm in the car," Stefan says.

I'm pouring gas in and out of Tori's car.

I toss an opened bottle of gas by Lina's gate.

I toss a burning shirt by the gate.

Fire spreads!

Tori's running.

I toss a match in the car.

I'm running.

I hear a car.

"Go!" I yell. Stefan speeds off.

Stefan pulls over so the ambulance and police can pass.

"Damn," Stefan says. "I wish I would've seen that shit."

"Shit, let's go back," Tori says. "I can get some footage so them bitches never forget this shit."

We go back to the crime scene.

Melissa, Lina and Erica are crying talking to the cops.

The neighbors are being nosy.

There's firefighters and police everywhere.

"You feel better now?" Tori asks on the way home. "I know you probably want to take someone away from them, but it's not worth it."

"On some real shit Natalie," Stefan says. "If you thinking about that shit, don't do it. Don't make no one pay for what them bitches did."

"Don't take a life period," Tori says. "That shit ain't cool. We got they asses now let God take care of the rest."

When we get to my house she says her boo is on the way.

"Tell him to chill here," I say. "I owe you. Let him come in and do you."

Stefan kisses my neck while I make the drinks.

"Girl come out here," Tori says. "Tyson this is my friend Natalie. Natalie this is Tyson."

"You were good in *Fools Back Out*," Tyson says. I say thank you.

"So where you want us to go?" Tori asks.

"Just have a good time," I say and take Stefan to my room.

He takes his shirt off.

I pull his pants down and put his dick in my mouth.

He takes my panties off.

He eats me.

I hear Tori moaning.

I'm walking panty-less.

Tyson's eating Tori's pussy on my counter.

"I need my drink," I say.

"No let's watch," Stefan says. He puts his dick in my ass while we watch Tori and Tyson fuck.

Me and Stefan go to my backhouse.

We cum again.

We're nosy again and Tori's giving Tyson head.

They see us.

They don't care.

I give Stefan head on the couch in front of them.

Tyson passes Stefan the blunt.

Tori rides Tyson.

Chester calls.

"Meet me at my place," Chester says.

I arrive to his place and he gets in my car. He pulls out his camera and Amber walks in the frame.

Now Melissa is.

Her and Amber are talking.

Melissa leaves and Lina and Erica walk in with masks on.

Lina and Erica beat the hell out of Amber.

Amber's face is bleeding.

"Your lies played a part in what we did to her," Lina tells Amber.

Erica's calling nine one one. "Our friend is trying to kill herself. We're in room twelve," Erica says. "Acting one on one," she says to Amber.

Erica and Lina drag Amber in the bathroom.

It sounds like they're banging her head on the counter.

Lina and Erica leave.

"Paramedics were in the wrong room," Chester says.

49

"Lovie what are you doing?" Melissa asks.

She's crying.

It's the eve of my birthday.

"Nothing," I say. "What's wrong?"

"Do you really forgive us?" Melissa asks.

"Yes. Why?" I ask.

"Jamal has the tape of us outside his house that night," Melissa says. "Lorena paid him but we know he has copies."

"I do," I say.

"I love you," Melissa says.

"I love you too," I say.

50

PRESTON WILKINS

Why does this bitch Amber try to act black? And have you guys ever heard of a Latoya Brown? She's passed around by celebrities.

    I release the video of Amber getting her ass beat.
    Lina has a mugshot.
    Erica has two.

51

I'm in the front burning Preston's body.
   I'm not sorry.
   Fear a patient woman.

SWEET REVENGE

Copyright by Roshinaie Johnson

ISBN: 978-0-9989873-2-3

Cover by Anna Fong

This book may not be copied.

There's no remorse.

www.ingramcontent.com/pod-product-compliance
Lightning Source LLC
Chambersburg PA
CBHW060357050426
42449CB00009B/1785